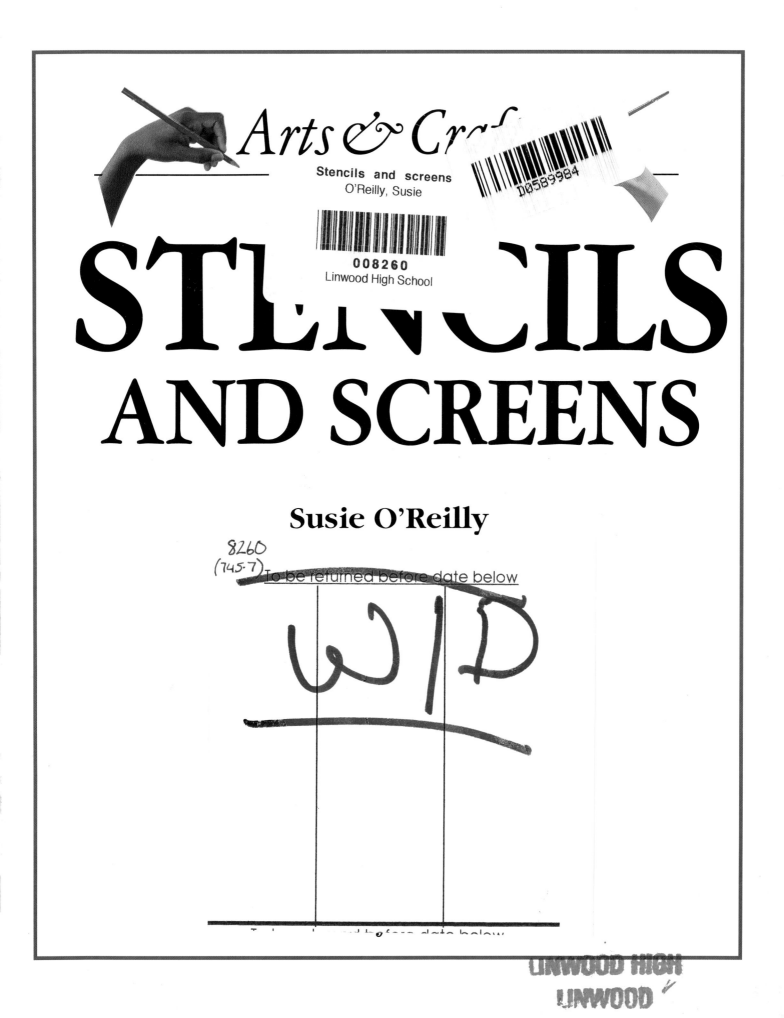

Arts & Craft

STENCILS
AND SCREENS

Susie O'Reilly

8260   (745.7)

Titles in this series

BATIK AND TIE-DYE
BLOCK PRINTING
KNITTING AND CROCHET
MODELLING
NEEDLECRAFT
PAPER MAKING
STENCILS AND SCREENS
WEAVING

*Frontispiece Alphabet stencils
designed and cut by schoolchildren
with the help of letterist
David Holgate.*

This edition published in 1994
by Wayland (Publishers) Ltd

© Copyright 1993 Wayland
(Publishers) Ltd

First published in 1993 by
Wayland (Publishers) Ltd
61 Western Road, Hove
East Sussex BN3 1JD, England

Editor: Anna Girling
Designer: Jean Wheeler

**British Library Cataloguing in
Publication Data**
O'Reilly, Susie
Stencils and Screens. – (Arts &
Crafts Series)
I. Title II. Series
745.7

HARDBACK ISBN 0-7502-0778-7

PAPERBACK ISBN 0-7502-1417-1

Typeset by Dorchester Typesetting
Group Ltd, Dorchester, Dorset, England
Printed and bound by Lego, Italy

CONTENTS

Words printed in **bold** appear in the glossary.

GETTING STARTED

Stencilling and screen printing are both simple ways of applying colour and pattern to a surface. Using these processes, you can make patterns which repeat the same **motif** over and over again, or you can make a number of identical prints. In both **techniques** certain areas of a design are masked out to block the colour from reaching the print surface, while the unmasked areas allow the colour through.

Stencilling is one of the oldest of all decorative techniques. It has been used since the **Stone Age**, although it only received its present name in the fifteenth century. The word 'stencil' comes from the medieval French word 'estenceler', which means to sparkle. It is a good way of describing the lively, light effect of a stencilled pattern.

Screen printing is put to all sorts of uses. This ▶ *man is printing a poster.*

▼ *Stencil brushes have short, stubby bristles.*

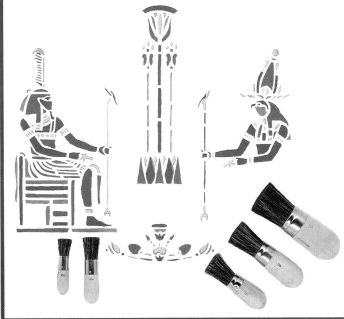

Screen printing is a development of stencilling. In screen printing the mask is held in place by a woven mesh. Ink is forced through the unmasked areas of the mesh giving a flat sheet of colour. The first screens were made of silk, so the technique was called silk screen printing. Now the mesh is usually made of cotton or **synthetic** material rather than silk.

Objects made in a wide range of materials, including paper, cardboard, wood, metal, plaster, glass, plastic, ceramic and cloth, can be decorated with screen printed and stencilled designs. Stencilling is mainly a hand process used by individual artists and craftspeople, but screen printing can be done by hand or machine, by artists, skilled printers or unskilled factory workers using computer-driven machinery. Screen printing is used on many of the things that you see and use every day, including posters, price tags and tickets, clothes and curtains, tiles, kettles and toasters, wallpapers and crockery.

▲ *Stencilling can be used to decorate a wall.*

To get started you will need these tools and materials.

General equipment:
Paper and card
Cloth (plain cotton is best)
Masking tape
Clear sticky tape
Newspapers
Paper tissues and towels
Craft knife
Cutting board
Scissors
Tracing paper
Metal ruler
Iron
Old plastic bowl
Rubber gloves
Overall
Pencils
Fine sandpaper
Varnish
Notebook and camera

For stencilling:
Oiled stencil paper (from art and craft shops)
Thin one-ply cardboard (the kind used for postcards)
Vegetable oil
Special stencil brushes with short stubby hairs (from art and craft shops)
Pieces of sponge
Quick-drying paints (e.g. poster and acrylic paints)

For screen printing:
Wooden frames (old picture frames are ideal)
Fine nylon mesh (e.g. old nylon net curtains)
Drawing pins and a small hammer
Brown paper gumstrip
Newsprint

Safety
Always be careful with knives. Use a special craft knife and ask an adult to set the blade so that it does not stick out far from the handle. Put the blade away safely when you have finished. Always press evenly while cutting and make sure the knife does not slip. Do not let your fingers get in the way of the blade.

Screen printing ink and binder (from craft shops) or wallpaper paste to add to poster paint
A **squeegee** (a plastic ruler, window or windscreen wiper, or strip of paper card or vinyl floor tile)
An old spoon
Cold-water dyes (e.g. Dylon cold-water dyes)

STENCILLING AROUND THE WORLD

Stencilling is an ancient art form that has been used by people all over the world. Early stencillers used whatever materials came easily to hand to make the stencils. Some examples of early stencilled patterns can still be seen, but the stencils themselves have not survived. Either they wore out in use, or disintegrated over time.

Examples of early stencilling can be found in some rock and cave paintings. The cave artists discovered that they could make an image by spraying colour through a hollow bone or plant stalk around the spread fingers of their hands. In this way, their own hands acted as very simple stencils.

In prehistoric times cave artists used their hands as stencils. These very old rock paintings are in Mexico. ▶

▼ *Blue* adire *cloth from West Africa.*

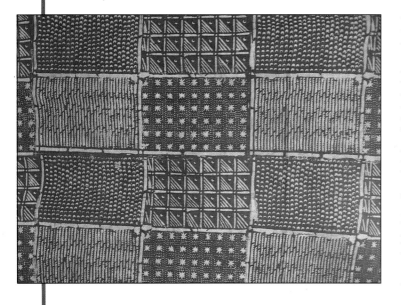

Fijian islanders, in the Pacific Ocean, traditionally decorate their clothing with simple stencils cut from bamboo and banana leaves. In West Africa, the Yoruba people use stencils to make *adire* cloth, which has light blue and white designs patterned on a blue background. They use sheets of pierced tin to apply patterns of flour paste on to cotton cloth before it is put in the dark blue dye. The dye does not colour the areas covered by paste. The Inuit people on Baffin Island use stencils cut from dried seal skin.

◀ *Japanese robes stencilled with bold designs.*

A stencilled ▶ bedroom from a house in Connecticut, USA.

Both the Japanese and Chinese have used stencilling for centuries. The Japanese discovered a way of making strong, **durable** stencils out of paper made from mulberry bush bark and waterproofed with a coating of **persimmon** juice. In the sixth and seventh centuries they decorated the leather armour of the **Samurai warriors** with stencilled decorations. By the nineteenth century, they had discovered a way to hold the different parts of a stencil together using a web of silk threads and human hair. They used these delicate stencils to print intricate pictures and patterns on fine silk.

The early European settlers in North America could not afford to carpet their floors, wallpaper their walls or to import fine furniture, so they used stencilling to decorate their houses.

In North America, ▶ *stencilling was a popular way of brightening up simple furniture. This American rocking chair dates from the first half of the nineteenth century.*

Some people did their own stencilling, but it was more usual to employ a decorator. These artists travelled from town to town working for anyone who could afford to pay their fees. They stencilled flowers, leaves, stars, birds, bells and pineapples in warm, earthy colours over pale grey, red or dark blue backgrounds. In 1818 Lambert Hitchcock set up a furniture stencilling factory in the little town of Barkhamsted, Connecticut. The work of his teams of stencillers, many of whom were women, become so well known that the town was nicknamed Hitchcockville.

By the time of the Second World War, plainer and simpler interiors were fashionable, and stencilling fell out of fashion. Recently there has been a great revival of the craft in Europe and North America. Stencilling is now seen as an art form and has been used to decorate expensive restaurants and hotels. Many people use stencilling in their homes.

CUTTING STENCILS

A good stencil design is made up of clean, bold shapes. The spaces between the shapes are as important as the shapes themselves. Use thin card to make your stencils. You can buy special stencil card from an art or craft shop, or you can use thin one-ply card – the sort used for postcards is about right.

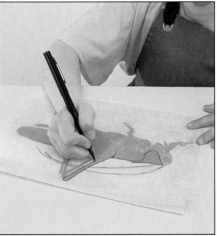

2 Make an accurate drawing of the design, then make a tracing of it on tracing paper.

1 Experiment with the design on pieces of scrap paper. Turn to pages 26-9 for some suggestions for starting points for designs and for advice on how to adapt these ideas to make stencils. Allow for good **bridges** of card between the cut out spaces. This makes not only a good design but also a strong stencil which will not break up in use. Leave at least a 12-cm margin all round the outside of the design so that the brush will not smudge paint over the edge when you are stencilling.

3 Tape the tracing firmly to the stencil card, using masking tape.

4 Now cut out the design, cutting through the tracing paper to the card. Use a cutting board and a sharp craft knife. **Remember: always be careful when using a craft knife. Ask an adult to help you. Use an even pressure as you cut.**

6 If you are using ordinary card, wipe a thin layer of vegetable oil over your stencil using a paper tissue. Let the oil dry. Oiling the card makes it stronger and more **flexible**. You do not need to oil the special stencil card as it has been oiled already.

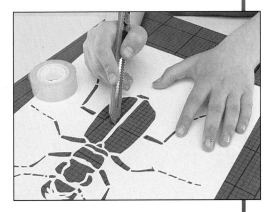

5 Start by cutting out the smallest spaces in your design. The card becomes weaker as more shapes are cut out, so you will have difficulty cutting fine shapes if you leave them until last.

7 If you tear one of the bridges of your stencil, repair it using a piece of clear sticky tape.

8 When you have finished stencilling, store your stencil flat in a folder.

MAKING A STENCILLED PRINT

A well-stencilled print has sharp, crisp outlines and soft, rich colours built up in layers. It is worth taking your time when stencilling to make sure you get a perfect result.

1 Place the object to be stencilled on a table covered with a layer of newspapers.

2 Think carefully about how you will position the stencil. The spaces above and below will play an important part in how it looks.

3 Tape the stencil to the surface using masking tape (masking tape can be peeled off afterwards and will not leave a mark).

4 Pour some paint on to a saucer. If possible, use a white saucer so that you can see the colour of the paint. Use quick-drying paint such as poster or acrylic paint. If you prefer, you can buy special fast-drying stencil paint from art and craft shops.

5 Dip your stencilling brush into the paint. Then dab it on a paper towel or newspaper to get rid of any excess paint. If you have too much paint on the brush it will run under the edges of the stencil.

7 When you have finished stencilling, remove all the masking tape from the stencils and gently wipe them clean. Wash the brushes out thoroughly and leave them to dry, bristles uppermost.

6 Hold the brush like a pencil, keeping it upright, with your fingers close to the bristles. Work the brush in broad, circular movements, clockwise and anti-clockwise, until the shapes are gradually filled in. Build up the colour slowly by applying several layers. Do not try to get a thick, rich effect using lots of paint all at once. You can also use pieces of sponge to dab on the paint.

▼ *Use stencils to make a repeating pattern – rather like wallpaper.*

MAKING A MULTICOLOURED PRINT

A multicoloured design can be built up using several stencils and overprinting using different coloured paints. A more detailed design can be made in this way.

1 Draw up a design using three colours and three stencils. The first stencil should give the main outline and background of the pattern. The second and third stencils will add detail.

2 If your design involves overprinting one colour on top of another, choose the palest colour for the first stencil and the darkest colour for the last.

3 Make a tracing for each colour and cut out the three separate stencils.

4 Check that the stencils will line up properly. Place each one in turn on top of another, and draw each outline through on to the stencil underneath, in pencil. If they do not line up, try again until you have a pencil outline for each stencil, correctly positioned.

5 Place all the stencils on top of one another, making sure each one matches its pencil outline. Cut away small triangles of card at the top, bottom and sides, cutting through all three stencils to make identical marks. These will be your **registration marks** and will help you position each stencil correctly.

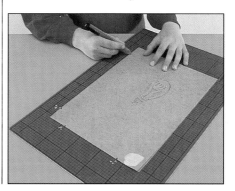

6 Stick the first stencil on the paper with masking tape. Use a pencil to mark in the triangular registration marks.

7 Make a print from your first stencil and allow the paint to dry completely.

8 Position the second stencil over the print. Move it around until all the registration marks show. This means the second stencil is in the correct position.

9 Make a print from the second stencil and allow the paint to dry completely.

10 Now position the third stencil, check the registration and print.

THE HISTORY OF SCREEN PRINTING

Screen printing is a very important printing technique. It is used widely by businesses and industry, as well as by artists. However, the technique was only discovered about a hundred years ago. In the 1870s, experiments were made to find a method of using a silk fabric screen to hold a stencil. The idea developed and in 1907 an Englishman called Samuel Simon applied for a **patent** for his technique of silk screen printing. At first, screen printing was used mainly by the **textile** industry to print patterned cloth quickly and cheaply. Soon the advertising, packaging and labelling industries started to use it to **mass-produce** banners, posters, cards and labels.

◀ *Screens can be used to hand print designs on to fabric.*

Around 1916, another method was developed. The screen was coated with a **gelatine** that was sensitive to light. Parts of the screen were then exposed to the light. The gelatine hardened in the parts that the light reached but could be washed away from the unexposed parts. The hardened gelatine acted like a stencil when ink was wiped over the screen.

At first, a paper stencil was attached to the underside of the screen. Later on, areas of the screen were painted with a varnish that would block the printing ink. Both these methods are still used by some hand screen printers today.

To begin with, artists were very reluctant to make use of the new technique of screen printing because a screen print was so unlike a painting. With paint and brushes they could create detailed and textured paintings, but screen printing produced bold designs, with large areas of plain colour and clean, crisp edges.

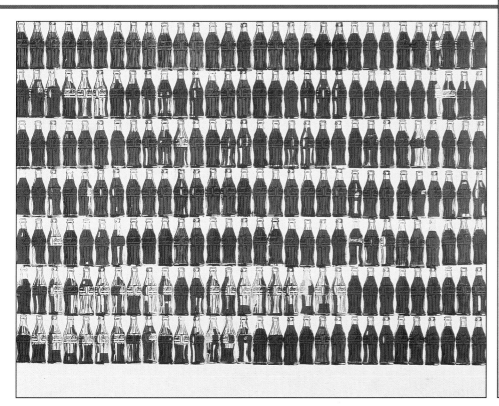

Screen printing was not widely used by artists until the 1960s. The American painter Andy Warhol used it to make pictures containing a series of identical images. Each print in the series was in a different **colour way.** He had been using rubber stamps, but realized that screen printing offered an ideal method of producing these 'multiples'. People were shocked by his prints of Coca-Cola bottles and soup cans. They felt that these ordinary, everyday things were not the right sort of subjects for works of art. However, many painters followed Warhol's example. Many experimental artists started to use screen printing in their work. Over the next thirty years screen printing developed as an important **medium** for artists.

▲ *Andy Warhol's Green Coca-Cola bottle (1962).*

▲ Green Dominance *(1977) by Bridget Riley. The artist uses screen printing to produce clean, crisp lines in her work.*

'Futurism' at Lenabo (1964) by Eduardo ▶ *Paolozzi. A different screen is used for each colour. How many different colours can you count?*

MAKING A SCREEN

Frames for screen printing are sold by art and craft shops and suppliers. You can make your own frame from strips of wood, or use a cardboard box with a hole cut in the bottom. Probably the best way to start is by finding a sturdy old picture frame with good, **rigid** corners.

1 Cut a piece of fine-mesh nylon netting, a little larger than the frame.

2 Wet the nylon and stretch it over the frame as tightly as possible.

3 Fix the mesh to the frame with drawing pins, using a small hammer. Start at the centre of one side and work a few centimetres to either side. Now turn to the opposite side of the frame and, pulling the nylon as tightly as you can, pin it opposite your first pin.

4 Do not finish either side yet, but pin the remaining two sides in the same way. Now work along each of the sides to the corners, pulling the nylon as tightly and evenly as you can. **Ask an adult to help you with the hammer and pins.**

5 Leave the nylon to dry. As it dries it will shrink. The screen must be stretched as tight as a drum, with no wrinkles.

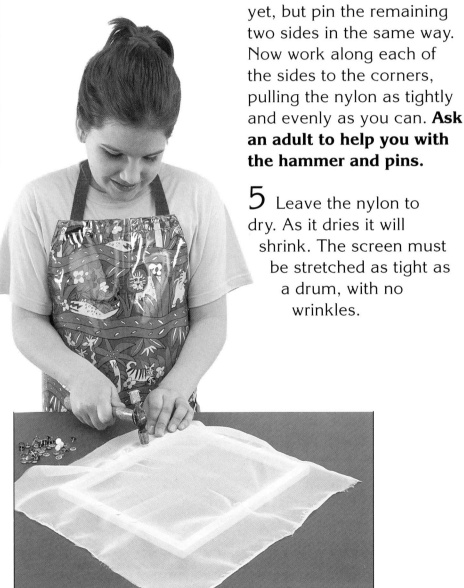

6 Trim the surplus netting from the edges of the screen with scissors. Then paste a layer of waterproof glue over the edges of the frame.

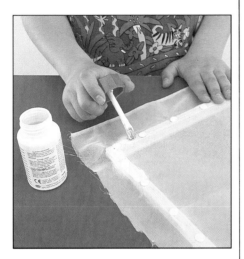

Cut four strips of gumstrip. Trim them to size and use them to mask the inside edges of the screen.

7 Lie the screen on the table, so the mesh is uppermost. Use brown paper gumstrip to mask the edges of the screen. Wet the gumstrip in a bowl of water before sticking it to the screen.

8 Now turn the screen over so that the mesh lies face down on the table.

This will stop the printing ink from spreading under the edge of the frame. It will also be used as the **reservoir** in which the pool of ink is held before it is pulled across the screen.

9 If you want to make a large number of prints it is a good idea to varnish over the tape with a waterproof varnish.

10 Clean the varnish off the brush using methylated spirit.

11 If the gumstrip starts to lift, use fresh strips to re-stick the edges of the screen and cover with varnish.

MAKING A SCREEN PRINT

1 Cover a table with an old, soft cloth or blanket. Over this, place a sheet of polythene covered with newspapers. Place a thick pad of newspaper in the centre of the table.

2 Cut a paper stencil from a sheet of newsprint. Turn to pages 26-7 for information on designing stencils.

3 Now prepare your printing ink. Mix up some wallpaper paste powder with water. Use half the water suggested on the packet so that the paste is quite thick. Wait until it becomes a clear jelly. Then add some poster paint or some dye powder dissolved in hot water. Alternatively, buy screen printing ink and binder (pictured below).

4 Find yourself a squeegee. You could use a window wiper, a flexible plastic ruler, or cut a strip from a vinyl floor tile. The squeegee must be slightly shorter in length than the width of the screen, but long enough to cover your design.

5 Now practise making a print. Put a test piece of printing paper on the newspaper pad. Put the stencil on the paper and place the screen over the stencil.

6 Spoon some of your printing ink on to the gumstrip reservoir at the side of the screen.

7 Ask a friend to hold the screen firmly on the table. Using your squeegee, pull the ink across the screen towards you. A good print has the same strength of colour throughout. It is made by sweeping the correct amount of ink across the screen in one even, non-stop movement. This will take practice.

8 Lift the screen off the print (the stencil will stick to the screen). Place the print on a flat surface to dry.

9 Make a second test print. You will probably find that the first prints are not very good. They will get better as the paper stencil becomes used to the wet ink.

10 Now make your actual print in exactly the same way. You can print on to paper or cloth. You can also take a number of prints from the screen. Keep your printing area tidy by removing any inky paper from your newspaper pad after each print.

11 When you have finished printing, wash the ink off the screen while it is still wet. Use washing-up liquid and a soft cloth.

If you let the ink dry on the screen it will clog up the holes in the mesh and you will not be able to use it again. Make sure you do not wash away the gumstrip edges. Leave the screen standing on its side to dry.

Screen Printing a T-Shirt

There is no limit to the range of designs which you can screen print on to a T-shirt. You might choose to print your name, or the name of a famous person, or simply an attractive pattern. You can use different screens to print different parts of the T-shirt.

1 Find a plain, light-coloured T-shirt. If it is new, wash it to get rid of the **finish**. The finish might stop the cloth from taking the ink.

2 Cut a piece of cardboard the size of the body of the T-shirt and slip it inside. This will stop the ink from the screen soaking through to the back of the shirt when you print the front.

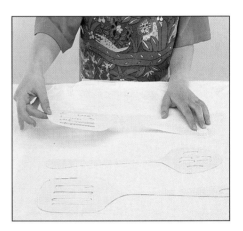

3 Prepare your paper stencils.

TURN TO PAGES 26-7 FOR INFORMATION ON DESIGNING STENCILS.

TURN TO PAGES 18-19 FOR INFORMATION ON SCREEN PRINTING.

4 Place the T-shirt on your printing pad and screen print your design. You will need to use screen printing ink made for printing on fabric. Alternatively, add a textile binder (from craft shops) to a cold-water dye such as Dylon.

5 When the T-shirt is dry, iron it with a cool iron to fix the colour. **Ask an adult to help you use the iron.**

▼ *Two T-shirt designs based on the same idea: the blue one uses a positive image and the red one a negative image (see page 26)*

Remember: your T-shirt must be washed separately. Some of the colour may run and stain other clothes.

CUTTING AN ALPHABET STENCIL

Letters make good stencils, because they are strong, simple shapes. Alphabet stencils are often used to spray names and instructions on to labels and packing cases. You can label things with your alphabet stencil or you can use it in making collages.

1 Start by collecting examples of different letter shapes. For example, look at newspapers and magazines, posters, carrier bags, cardboard boxes, food packets and shop and road signs. Look at the cover of this book! You will discover that there are lots of different ways of forming the same letter.

2 A good way of finding a variety of letters is to print out alphabets in different **founts** on a word processor.

3 Choose some of the letters and use a photocopier to enlarge them.

4 Design and cut stencils using the enlarged letters as the basis of your design. Trace the shapes using tracing paper. Think about the bridges you will need.

5 Different designs can be used to stencil the same letter. Experiment with the shapes. For example, the picture above shows ten different ways to stencil the letter 'O'.

6 Design the other letters of the alphabet and cut stencils for them. There are twenty-six letters, so ask some friends to help you.

8 Another idea is to make just a few letters and use them to make a picture. You can stencil the letters any way you like – on their side, or at an angle. Experiment and have fun.

7 If you want to write words for labels, make sure you position each letter carefully next to the one before, so that they sit on a straight line.

DECORATING A BOX

Stencilling is an ideal way to decorate a box. Boxes have three **dimensions**, so there are many surfaces to decorate. They can be picked up and turned round to give different views. The box will be opened and sometimes people will look underneath it. You need to think about how the outside and the inside decoration go together. You also need to think about what the box is going to contain. Can you make the design tell you something about the contents, or about the person who will own the box?

2 Decide on a stencil design for the box and make the stencils you will need.

3 Strip off any paper labels. Use fine sandpaper to rub the box down. The wood needs to be smooth all over.

1 Find a small wooden box – a tea, cheese or stationery box will be ideal.

Be careful not to breathe in any dust.

4 Paint an undercoat on to the wood using poster paint. The paint must cover the box smoothly and not let any old marking show through.

5 Once the paint is dry, sand the box again lightly. Then give the wood a second undercoat.

6 Before you start stencilling, try putting the stencils in different positions. This will help you decide where to place them to create the best effect on your box.

7 Stencil the design on the box.

8 Add extra decorative details using a paint brush if you wish.

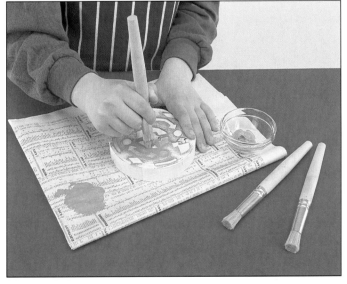

9 Give the box several coats of varnish to protect its surface. Let the varnish dry between each coat.

DESIGNING STENCILS

A stencilled design is made up of **positive** shapes
(the areas which are cut out to take the paint) and **negative** shapes
(the areas which block the paint). In a good design, these shapes,
and the bridges that hold the stencil in one piece work well together.

DESIGNING A STENCIL

4 Trace over the sketch. Try to improve the shapes, making the outlines crisper.

5 Trace over your tracing. Keep working on the design until you are really pleased with it. When you have cut out the stencil you can get an idea of how it will look when it is printed by placing it on a plain, coloured background.

1 Look around for some ideas for your design (see pages 28-9). Try a simple design at first.

2 Think carefully about which details will make positive shapes and which will make negative shapes. It is important to spend some time deciding where the bridges will need to go and how wide to make them. The bridges add strength to the stencil and hold together parts of the design but they must also blend in with the overall design.

3 Make a first sketch. Try to make each shape as bold as possible.

MAKING A QUICK STENCIL

This method works for square, rectangular and round stencils.

1 Fold a piece of paper in four.

2 Cut or tear out pieces from the sides.

3 Unfold the paper.

MAKING A MORE COMPLICATED STENCIL

This method works for square or round stencils.

1 Fold a piece of paper in four, and then again, diagonally, into a triangle.

2 Draw a pattern on the triangle of paper.

3 Cut out the pattern. Be careful not to cut along the fold lines or your stencil will fall apart.

4 Unfold the paper.

THE GALLERY

All sorts of natural, handmade and **manufactured** objects can give you ideas for stencilling and screen printing. Keep your camera or sketch book at the ready to record things you discover which have a good strong **silhouette,** or are made up of strong blocks of even colour. Shapes that can be simplified easily make good stencil designs. Flowers, plants and insects make good subjects for stencils because it is easy to blend the bridges into the overall design. While you are looking at shapes, make a note of which colours go well together too.

▲ *Stripy zebra skins.*

◀ *Apples with big shadows.*

▼ *The silhouette of a tractor.*

▲ Leaf shapes against the sky.

▼ The pattern of a carved window.

▲ Washing on a line.

A dahlia flower. ▶

▼ Stork silhouettes and their reflections.

GLOSSARY

Bridges In stencil making, the areas of card holding the different parts of the design together. They are usually narrow strips of card between the main, bold shapes.

Colour way In printing, the same design can be printed in a number of different colour combinations. Each of these is called a colour way.

Dimensions The measurements of an object in each direction. A three-dimensional object has height, depth and width.

Durable Long-lasting.

Finish The special surface put on cloth when it is made, to change the way it looks and feels.

Flexible Able to bend without breaking or cracking.

Fount A complete set of type – the alphabet, numbers, etc – which is all in the same style and size.

Gelatine A substance made by boiling up animal bones. It is used in food to make jelly and in glue to make it sticky.

Manufactured Made in large quantities, usually by machine in a factory.

Mass-produce To manufacture a very large quantity of the same object.

Medium A type of art, such as screen printing or sculpture or photography, which can be described by the particular techniques and materials used. Works of art are often grouped according to the medium by which they have been produced.

Motif A shape, usually quite small, that is repeated to make a pattern.

Negative The opposite of positive. In a stencil design, the negative is the area of card which blocks the paint.

Newsprint The special name for the type of low-quality paper that newspapers are printed on.

Patent A legal document giving an inventor the right to use his invention and stopping other people using it.

Persimmon A fruit which grows in tropical parts of the world.

Positive The opposite of negative. In a stencil design, the positive is the shape cut out to form the pattern. It is the area which lets the paint through.

Registration marks Marks which show a printer how to position a printing plate or stencil correctly. They are used when printing a design with more than one colour. The registration marks for each colour are lined up so that all the parts of the design fit together properly.

Reservoir An area that holds liquid. In screen printing, it is the part of the screen that holds the ink.

Rigid Unable to move.

Samurai warriors The fierce soldiers who formed the armies of Japan until the nineteenth century.

Silhouette The outline of a solid figure.

Squeegee A special tool used in screen printing to sweep ink evenly across the screen.

Stone Age A period of history many thousands of years ago. It is called the Stone Age because the early people of this time used stones to make tools.

Symmetrical Having two halves that are mirror images of each other.

Synthetic Made from chemicals; not natural.

Techniques Methods or skills.

Textiles All kinds of cloth, or the threads used to make cloth.

Further Information

Books to Read

Devonshire, Hilary *Printing* (Franklin Watts, 1991)

Nicholls, Frank *Stencils* (Child's Play, 1976, re-issue 1993)

Tofts, Hannah *The Print Book* (Franklin Watts, 1990)

Walton, Sally and Stewart *Stencil It!* (Simon and Schuster, 1992)

Places to Visit

Britain
The American Museum in
 Britain
Claverton Manor
Bath

The Tate Gallery
Millbank
London
SW1P 4RG

For further information about arts and crafts, contact the following organizations:

The Crafts Council
44A Pentonville Road
London
N1 9BY
UK

Crafts Council of New
 Zealand
22 The Terrace
Wellington
PO Box 498
Wellington Island
New Zealand

INDEX

ACKNOWLEDGEMENTS

The publishers would like to thank the following for allowing their photographs to be reproduced: American Museum in Britain 7 bottom; Bridgeman Art Library 7 top right, 15 all; Crafts Council frontispiece (E. Barber); Eye Ubiquitous 5 (P. Seheult), 7 top left (F. Leather), 14, 29 inset centre (J. Stephens); Hutchison Library 6 left (J. Highet Brimah); Tony Stone Worldwide 28 left (P. McArthur); Topham 4 left; Zefa 4 right, 6 right, 28 top right (F. Lanting), 28 bottom right (B. Peterson), 29 top left, 29 top right (R. Minsart), 29 bottom left, 29 bottom right (F. Lanting). All other photographs were supplied by Zul Mukhida. Logo artwork was supplied by John Yates.

The print *Green Dominance* (1977), by Bridget Riley, on page 15, appears by kind permission of the artist. The print *Green Coca-Cola bottle* (1962), by Andy Warhol, on page 15, appears by permission of the copyright holders: © 1993 The Andy Warhol Foundation for the Visual Arts Inc. The publishers have made every attempt to contact the artist Eduardo Paolozzi for permission to reproduce the print *'Futurism' at Lenabo* (1964) on page 15.

The publishers would like to thank Shirley Chubb for providing the screen print photographed for the cover border and inside covers.

The author would like to thank Jan Peek, Jackie Lee and Sarah Mossop for their help.